AuthorHouse™
1663 Liberty Drive, Suite 200
Bloomington, IN 47403
www.authorhouse.com
Phone: 1-800-839-8640

First published by AuthorHouse   10/29/2008

ISBN: 978-1-4389-2380-2 (sc)

Printed in the United States of America
Bloomington, Indiana

This book is printed on acid-free paper.

author HOUSE®

A Culinary Journey Thru Advent

25 secret ingredients

Christmas is almost here. It begins to snow and everybody wants a cozy atmosphere to create. Nothing is simpler, than achieving this with the preparation of traditional Christmas recipes.

The book shows one Advent calendar with 25 secret ingredients and 25 recipes - one surprise for each day of the Advent season.

25 classic ingredients - another spicy aroma and tasty flavor for each day. Cookies, cakes, hot punch and solid meals, which smell fabulous throughout the entire house. Enchant friends and family with unique Christmassy aromas and create therewith a warm and fuzzy feeling around everybody`s heart.

Like in grandmother`s times.

The recipes will bring you the winter nearer. Ring in the Christmastime.

Enjoy the book with all the Christmassy treats and thereby feel the Christmas spirit.

Snowflakes alighted, silent, the world gets covered in snow.

The glorious scenic winter landscape send out the celestial peace.

In the distance, chime the bells, dream-like.

Live together in the warmness of the kitchen, joyfully.

Fabulous smells enchant the world, heart-warming.

Ice, snow - everywhere. Beyond all questions: It's Christmastime.

This is for my husband, Hendrik,
who always believes in me.
And for my parents, without whose support
the book would not have been possible.

Contents

Gingerbread Advent Calendar

Gingerbread, in several variations, is primary served in the Advent season and at Christmastime. Gingerbread can have a cake or a cookie form. The cake is a spice cake, which you can serve warm with some kind of sauce, for example lemon sauce or vanilla sauce. Meanwhile the cookies are often cut into shapes; thin and crispy baked. Traditionally, honey is used for sweetening. Another important ingredient are the spices, especially cinnamon and clove. Very often the gingerbread becomes refined with candied orange peel, candied lemon peel, nuts, raisins or chocolate. The gingerbread is popular around the world. Try out this extraordinary recipe:

(16x12x1)

2/3 cup sugar beet molasses	1 cup flour
1/4 cup honey	2 tablespoons baking powder
1/3 cup unsalted butter	2 tablespoons cacao
	1/3 cup milk
2 eggs	3.5 oz. milk chocolate, grated
2 teaspoons cinnamon	1/2 cup candied orange peel
1/2 teaspoon ground clove	
zest of 1 lemon	gel food colors

In a saucepan, warm the molasses, the honey and the butter. Pour the mixture into a bowl and let it cool down.

Preheat the oven at 350°F.

For the gingerbread dough, mix the chilled molasses mixture with the eggs and the spices. Combine the dry ingredients (the flour, the baking powder and the cacao). Add it to the mixture and stir well. Mix in the milk.

Finally, fold in the grated chocolate and the candied orange peel.

Pour the gingerbread dough into an oiled baking pan. Then bake the gingerbread for about 20 minutes. Let it cool down. Then decorate it with gel food colors. First, draw the 25 small boxes. Then decorate them with the numbers. In this way, you get an Advent calendar.

December 2nd

Smoked turkey pastries

Ginger is a plant species. Ginger grows in the tropics and subtropics, like India, China, South America and Australia. For the main part, the ginger roots are used in the kitchen. Ginger is well-known in the Asian cuisine. Generally, the spice is popular in the cookery and in the bakery. In this recipe ginger is combined with other strong aromas:

(8 pieces)

17.3 oz. puff pastry (2 sheets, defrosted)

1 lb green asparagus

5 oz. smoked turkey breast, slices

1/3 cup orange juice

1/1/2 tablespoons all-purpose flour

zest of 1 orange

1 teaspoon ginger, grated

salt, pepper, nutmeg

1 egg

1 tablespoon milk

Cut off the ligneous ends of the asparagus. Then cut the asparagus into 1 inch pieces. Bring a pot with salted water to a boil and blanch the asparagus pieces for about 3 minutes in it. After it refresh the asparagus pieces and drain them.

Cut the turkey breast slices into cubes.

For the sauce, whisk the orange juice and the flour. Add the orange zest and the ginger. Season to taste with salt, pepper and nutmeg. Combine the sauce with the asparagus pieces and the turkey cubes. Stir well.

Lightly roll each sheet of puff pastry to a square. Then cut each sheet into four smaller squares.

Preheat the oven at 400°F.

Whisk the egg with the milk. Brush the edges of each square with it. Place about 1/3 cup of the asparagus-turkey mixture on each square. Fold the squares diagonally, so that you get triangles. Seal the pastries by pressing the edges with a fork.

Place the small pastries on a baking sheet. Use parchment paper. Brush the tops with the egg mixture and make 2 slits with a sharp knife.

Bake the pastries about 20 minutes until they are lightly brown. Serve the pastries warm.

December 3rd

Vanilla kipferl

Vanilla is widely grown throughout the tropics. The world`s largest producer is Madagascar. Vanilla stems from an orchid. The vanilla bean grows quickly on the vine and is ready for harvest after 9 month. The harvest is before full ripeness, so that the vanilla beans don`t open. Altogether, there are three preparations of natural vanilla: you can use the whole pod, vanilla powder/sugar or vanilla extract. Vanilla is used to sweeten meals and desserts. Try out this traditional German recipe:

(40 pieces)

7 oz. unsalted butter

1/1/4 cup flour

1/4 teaspoon baking powder

4 oz. ground almonds

1/3 cup sugar

1 vanilla pod

1/3 cup sugar

2 tablespoons natural Vanilla Sugar

In a mixing bowl, mix up all ingredients. Scratch out the vanilla pod and add the vanilla to the other ingredients. Knead a cookie dough. Wrap the dough into plastic wrap and put it in the fridge for 30 minutes. Then form a roll (1 inch in diameter). Cut the roll into 3/4 inch pieces. Form small half moons and place them on a baking sheet. Use parchment paper. Bake them about 15 minutes at 340°F. Meanwhile, mix up the remaining sugar and the Vanilla Sugar. Roll the hot cookies in it. Let them cool down.

Black salsifies with fish fillet

Black salsifies arise from the Iberian Peninsula (Spain). In the 17th century they came to the rest of Europe. Even today, Europe, or rather Belgium, France and the Netherlands are the world`s largest producer. In the wintertime, the longish roots are a popular vegetable. This is why the black salsify has also the name "winter asparagus".

(4 servings)

1 cup milk	salt, peppcr
2 lb. black salsifies	4 pieces walleye with skin (4 x 8 oz.)
2 tablespoons butter	salt, pepper
2 tablespoons powdered sugar	2 tablespoons butter

In a large bowl, combine the milk with 2 cups of water. Wash the black salsifies, then peel them and cut off the ends. Then lay the black salsifies into the milk mixture, so that they are covered with it. In this way they don`t turn brown.

Drain the black salsifies. Cut them into 1/8 inch slices. Warm the butter in a pan and stew the slices over a medium heat for 6 to 8 minutes. After it, besprinkle the black salsifies with powdered sugar and let them caramelize. Season to taste with salt and pepper.

Season the fish fillets with salt and pepper. Warm the butter and the olive oil in a big pan. Fry the fish with the skin downward for about 4 to 5 minutes in it. Then turn the fish round and fry the fillets for another 2 to 3 minutes.

Serve with black salsifies.

Poppy Stollen

Poppy isn't only a gorgeous flower with a variety of colors. The culinary uses are also a highlight. Poppy is widely consumed in Central and Eastern Europe, mostly in the form of sweet dishes. The poppy seeds are boiled with milk and used as filling for sweet pastries. The following recipe is a traditional sweet pastry of Silesia (Poland):

(1 loaf)

2 cups flour

2 teaspoons baking powder

4 oz. butter

2 eggs

1/2 cup sugar

1 tablespoon rum

1 cup quark

1/4 cup candied orange peel

1/2 cup almonds, hacked

2/3 cup raisins

1 tablespoon rum

1 cup milk

1 cup poppy seeds, milled

2 eggs

1/4 cup sugar

1/4 cup ground almonds

2 tablespoons cream

2 oz. soft butter

1/4 cup powdered sugar

For the dough, sieve the flour and the baking powder into a large bowl. Add the butter, the eggs, the sugar and the rum. Drain the quark through a towel; the towel will sponge up the liquid. Then add it to the other ingredients. Combine the ingredients. Then add the candied orange peel and the almonds. Knead a smooth dough. Let the dough rest for about an hour.

Meanwhile, hack the raisins. Pour the rum over the raisins and let it steep for at least 20 to 30 minutes. Bring the milk to a boil and pour it over the poppy seeds. Let the mixture cool down. Batter the eggs and the sugar. Stir in the poppy mixture. Add the ground almonds and the rum raisins. Stir everything well.

On a floured surface, roll the dough rectangular about 3/4 inch thin. Spread it with the poppy filling. Furl both longer sides equal, until they meet in the center. Place the "Stollen" with the interface downward on a baking sheet.

Preheat the oven at 375°F.

Brush the "Stollen" with the cream and bake it for 60 to 70 minutes. Let it cool down a little bit. Then brush it with the soft butter and besprinkle it with powdered sugar.

Stutenkerle

The "Stutenkerl" is a German tradition in the pre-Christmas period. He`s made from sweetened yeast dough. He`ll decorated with raisins for the face and the button border. By a religious tradition the "Stutenkerl" symbolizes a bishop, named Saint Nicholas (4. cent.). Even today he`ll baked at St. Nicholas` Day, December 6th.

(6 pieces)

3 oz. unsalted butter

2/3 cup milk

2 cups plain flour

1 envelope dry yeast

1/4 teaspoon salt

1/3 cup sugar

1 egg

1 egg egg-white

raisins

1 egg yolk

In a saucepan, warm the butter and the milk. In a large bowl, mix the flour, the dry yeast, the salt, the sugar, the egg and the egg white. Pour the milk-butter mixture over it and knead a smooth yeast dough. Place the dough in a bowl and cover it with a towel. Let it prove for about an hour.

Cut a stencil about 10 inch sized (see page 16). Roll the dough on a floured surface about 1/2 inch thin. Place the stencil on the dough and cut out the "Stutenkerle". Lay them on a baking sheet. Use parchment paper.

Decorate the "Stutenkerle" with raisins. Whisk the egg yolk and the milk. Brush them with it. Then let them prove another 20 minutes. Preheat the oven at 350°F. Bake the "Stutenkerle" for 20 minutes. Let them cool down.

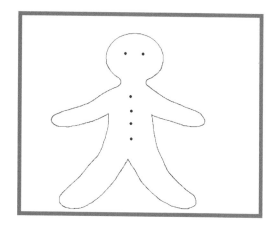

Stencil: 10 inch sized

Kale with smoked pork chop

Kale is a typical winter vegetable. It prefers cooler climates. The most important growing areas are Europe and North America. If the kale is harvested after the first frost, it tastes sweeter and more flavorful. The kale meal is a tradition in northern Germany and in parts of Scandinavia. The following is a traditional recipe:

(4 servings)

2 lb. fresh kale, chopped

2 yellow onions, finely chopped

2 tablespoons butter

1/4 cup dry red wine

2 cups chicken broth

salt

2 tablespoons mustard

2 lb. boneless smoked pork chops

Blanch the kale for about 3 minutes in salted boiling water. Then refresh the kale and drain it. In a big pot, stew the onions in the butter for about 2 minutes. Add the kale and braise everything for another 5 minutes. Pour the red wine over it and let it boil down. Then pour the broth over it and season to taste with salt and mustard. Let the kale simmer over a low heat for about 1 hour. After 45 minutes add the boneless smoked pork chops, so that they can cook in the kale. Serve with boiled potatoes.

Winter punch

"Gluehwein" is an hot alcoholic beverage, which traditionally in Central Europe to the Christmas season is drunk; often on Christmas markets. The main ingredient, white wine or red wine, is warmed up with different spices, traditionally with cinnamon, clove, lemon peel and star anise. It is very important that you don`t bring the wine to a boil, because the alcohol fast evaporates. You can vary the "Gluehwein" and prepare a punch: add rum, brandy or a liqueur, like amaretto. Or just vary your punch with juices:

(1 liter)

1 bottle (0.75 l) dry white wine

2 cups white cranberry juice

1/4 cup rock sugar (white)

3 whole star anis

4 cloves

1 cinnamon stick

Combine all ingredients in a pot. Bring it almost to a boil.

Take the punch off the heat and let it steep for about 30 minutes.

Serve the punch warm. If desired, rewarm the punch a little bit.

Cabbage pastries with tea punch

Cabbage is a popular vegetable in Autumn and in Winter. From the early varieties to the late cabbage, it matures in between 45 and 87 days. The leader in production is China, followed by India and Russia. The US-production is also under the Top-10. You can store cabbage a long time. The ways of cooking are varied: you can cook stews or soups, prepare sauerkraut or just use the cabbage raw for a salad. Here`s another extraordinary idea of preparing a delicious cabbage dish:

Tea punch

(1 liter)

1 liter black tea

1/4 cup brown sugar

2 lemons, cut into thin slices

8 cloves

Put everything together in a saucepan and bring it to a boil. Put it off the heat and let it steep for about 15 minutes. Garnish the glasses with the lemon slices.

Cabbage pastries

(12 pieces)

1 cup plain flour

1/4 teaspoon salt

4 oz. unsalted butter

1 egg

2 tablespoons milk

10 oz. cabbage, cut into thin ribbons

1 bunch Italian parsley, hacked

1 tablespoon olive oil

3 eggs

2/3 cup cream

4 oz. crumbled blue cheese

salt, pepper

In a large bowl, combine the flour, the salt, the butter, the egg and the milk. Knead quickly a short pastry. Wrap the dough into plastic wrap and put it into the fridge for about one hour. On a floured surface, roll the short pastry very thin. Use a small bowl or a glass (5.5 inch in diameter) and prick out 12 circles. Butter a muffin pan and fill each hollow with a pastry circle. Press the pastry on the rim of the form. With a fork, prick several holes into the pastry bottom.

Preheat the oven at 400°F.

In a pan, warm the olive oil. Stew the cabbage about 5 minutes in it. Add the parsley. Fill the pastries with the cabbage.

Whisk together the eggs and the cream. Stir in the blue cheese and season to taste with salt and pepper. Pour the mix over the pastries. Bake them for 20 to 25 minutes. Serve them warm.

Quark - eggnog dessert

Eggnog is an alcoholic beverage made of eggs, milk or cream and alcohol (rum, brandy or whiskey). There is the cold and the hot variant, which is drunk only in winter. In the 19 century became eggnog the traditional beverage for Christmas and New Year. In Great Britain it is also very popular. Enclosed I will show you, that you can also prepare a wonderful dessert with eggnog.

(4 to 6 servings)

10 oz. canned cherries, drained

1 cup quark

1/4 cup sugar

1/2 cup cream

1/2 cup eggnog

2 oz. chocolate sprinkles

Dependently of, how large the glasses or how small the bowls are, you can prepare 4 to 6 servings.

Arrange the cherries in the glasses.

Mix up the quark with the sugar. Whip and fold in the cream. Arrange the mixture on the cherries.

Pour the eggnog over the quark (instead you can also use vanilla sauce).

Strew the chocolate sprinkles over the desserts.

Put the desserts into the fridge for at least 5 hours.

Fig chutney with cheese

Figs occur in many species and colors. You can eat the fig raw with cheese, prosciutto or in salads. You can also prepare sweet dishes with figs. You can keep the dried figs up to 12 month. You can eat the figs as they are or just stew them for about 20 minutes in water until they are soft. Try out this delicious recipe:

(4 to 6 servings)

1 tablespoon olive oil

1/2 cup yellow onions, diced

1/1/2 lb. figs

2 tablespoons dry red wine

1/3 cup balsamic vinegar

1/4 cup red wine vinegar

1/2 cup water

8 sage leaves

1/4 teaspoon ground red pepper

1/4 cup honey

2 teaspoons brown sugar

Warm the olive oil in a saucepan. Stew the onions for 2 minutes in it. Cut the figs into pieces and add them to the onions. Stew for another 3 minutes. Pour the red wine over it and let it boil down. Now, pour the vinegars and the water over it. Add the sage leaves (When you close them up in a tea ball, you can remove them very easy), the ground red pepper, the honey and the sugar.

Let the mixture simmer over a medium heat for about an hour. After half an hour remove the sage.

Serve the fig chutney warm or cold. Serve with cheese and crackers.

Black & White cookies

Cacao is made of the seed of the cacao tree. The key growing areas are Central America and Africa. You can make a drinking chocolate with it: Just mix it up with hot milk or with hot water and a bit of sugar. You can also bake with cacao. Try out this recipe, which makes every cookie individual:

(70 pieces)

1/2 cup unsalted butter

1/3 cup sugar

2 tablespoons powdered sugar

1 egg

1/1/2 cups self-rising flour

1/1/2 tablespoons sweet ground chocolate

1 teaspoon milk

Batter the butter, the sugar, the powdered sugar and the egg. Add the flour and knead a cookie dough. Halve the dough. Knead in the sweet ground chocolate and the milk into one half. Wrap both cookie dough into plastic wrap and put it in the fridge for 1 hour.

Preheat the oven at 350°F. Roll each dough on a floured surface (12 x 8 inch). Lay one dough on top of the other. Now roll out the dough very thin (about 1/8 inch) and furl it lengthwise. The roll should have a diameter of 1 inch. Cut the roll into 1/4 inch pieces and put them on a baking sheet. Use parchment paper. Bake the cookies for about 12 minutes. Then cool them down on a cooling rack.

Oven broiled vegetables

Cardamom originates from India and Sri Lanka. Even today, India is the largest exporting country. The cardamom seeds contain essential oils, which give them the spicy, sweet-hot aroma. Cardamom is widespread in Asian countries. Cardamom is an ingredient of many seasonings. It is often used in curries. In the European cuisine, by contrast, it is often used in the Christmas bakery and other baked goods.

1/3 cup olive oil

1 teaspoon orange zest

juice of 1 orange

1/1/2 teaspoons cardamom

1/4 teaspoon ground red pepper

salt, pepper

2 fennels

4 fresh artichokes

3 oz. black olives, cut into halves

4 oz. feta, crumbled

For the vinaigrette, whisk the olive oil with the orange zest, the orange juice, the cardamom and the ground red pepper. Season with salt and pepper.

Cut the fennels lengthwise into 1/8 thin stripes. Hack the green leaves of the fennel and keep it.

Cut of the upper third of the artichokes. Peel off the dark and hard outer leaves of the artichokes. Trim the stems. Then peel the dark green areas from the stem and the base of the artichokes. Halve the artichokes and cut them into smaller pieces.

Combine the fennel, the artichokes and the olives with the vinaigrette. Pour the vegetables onto a baking sheet.

Preheat the oven at 400°F

Broil the vegetables for about 15 minutes. Then strew the feta over the vegetables and broil it for another 10 minutes.

Bestrew the vegetables with the hacked fennel leaves and serve immediately.

Plaited yeast bun with marzipan and almonds

Marzipan is a treat, which is generally made of almonds and sugar. Ground almonds, powdered sugar and other aromas, such as rosewater, are heated up at about 200 °F for about 30 to 40 minutes. But the exact recipes of each manufacturer are company secrets. Who invented the marzipan, is not clarified until today: either it was invented in Germany or in Estonia. Today the "Luebecker Marzipan" is world-famous.

(1 loaf)

2/3/4 cups flour

2 envelopes dried-yeast

1/2 cup sugar

salt

4 oz. unsalted butter, melted

1/1/4 cup milk, warm

2 oz. butter, soft

4 oz. marzipan

2. oz sour cream

1 tablespoon sugar

1/4 teaspoon cinnamon

2. oz sliced almonds

For the yeast dough, combine the flour and the yeast. Add the sugar, a dash of salt, the melted butter and the warm milk. Knead a smooth dough. Cover the dough with a towel and let it prove about 1 hour. After it divide the dough into three equal pieces in size. Now, prepare two plaited loaves, a big one with two pieces yeast dough and a smaller one with the remaining piece of yeast dough. Both plaited loaves should be 12 inch in length.

For the filling, combine the butter and the marzipan. Spread the mixture on the larger plaited loaf. Lay the smaller one on top. Place it on a baking sheet and let it prove for another 30 minutes.

Preheat the oven at 375°F. Mix up the sour cream, the sugar and the cinnamon. Brush the plaited loaf with it and bestrew it with the sliced almonds. Bake it for about 45 minutes.

Turnip stew

Turnips are root vegetables. The turnips were rediscovered in Scandinavia in the 17 century. The actual origin is unknown. The turnip is a winter vegetable. It is cultivated in temperate climates. Actually, the harvest season is from September to May. The turnip is versatile: You can cook stews, soups and purees.

(6 serving)

2 tablespoons vegetable oil

1 lb. beef stew meat, cut into 1 inch cubes

2 yellow onions, cubed

1/3 cup dry red wine

salt, pepper

8 cups vegetable stock

3 bay leaves

1 lb. yukon gold potatoes, peeled and cubed

1/2 lb. golden beets, peeled and cubed

1 lb. turnips, peeled and cubed

Warm the oil in a big pot. Over a medium heat, braise the meat for about 3 minutes in it. Add the onions and stew for another 2 minutes.

Pour the red wine over it and let it boil down. Season the meat with salt and pepper. Add 4 cups of the vegetable stock. Let it simmer over a medium heat for about 30 minutes.

Add the bay leaves, the potatoes, the golden beets and the turnips. Pour the remaining stock over it. Put a lid on the pot and let the soup simmer for another 20 to 25 minutes.

If you like bestrew the stew with hacked parsley and serve immediately.

Rice pudding with blueberries

Blueberries are native only to North America. Particularly, blueberries are cultivated and grown wild. The wild grown blueberries are smaller, but have an more intense flavor. The blueberry production in North America starts in mid May and ends in September. Otherwise the southern hemisphere gives different periods for the growing season. In South America, for example, the harvest begins in Winter and continues to mid-March. Blueberries are delicious and sweet. You can use them diversified in the cuisine: cook jellies, bake pies or muffins are just eat them raw. This is another delicious idea:

(4 servings)

4 cups milk

salt

1/4 cup sugar

2 teaspoons lemon zest

2/3 cup short grain rice

4 cups blueberries

1/1/4 cups blueberry nectar

2 tablespoons custard powder

In a pot, bring the milk, a dash of salt, the sugar and the lemon zest to a boil. Add the rice and let it simmer over a medium heat for about 30 to 35 minutes. Let the rice pudding cool down a bit.

In a saucepan, bring the nectar to a boil. Add the blueberries, but keep 1/2 cup. Let the blueberries simmer over a medium heat for about 10 minutes. Stir in the custard powder. Let it cool down a bit.

Arrange the rice pudding with the blueberries in glasses and garnish with the remaining berries. Put it into the fridge for at least 3 hours.

Herring salad

In Europe the clove is well-known since the Middle Ages. The spice spread out through Europe and Asia. The clove is the dried flower bud of a tree, which is native on the Spice Islands. Today, the clove is cultivated around the world. The clove is very aromatic and has a hot flavor. The spice contains essential oils, from which arises the wonderful, unique flavor. The spice is used for baking, often in the Christmastime and for the cookery, to marinade fish or meat or to prepare sauces.

(4 servings)

12 oz. beets

12 oz. herring, cut into pieces

1 red onion, diced

1/2 apple, diced

3 oz. pickles, diced

2 tablespoons walnuts, hacked

8 oz. sour cream

3/4 teaspoon ground clove

1 tablespoon apple cider vinegar

1 teaspoon sugar

salt, pepper

Cut off the leaves of the beets. Place the beets in a big pot with salted water and bring it to a boil. Then let it simmer over a medium heat for 40 minutes. Let them cool down. Now peel and dice the beets. Combine the beets with all other ingredients.

For the salad dressing, whisk the sour cream with the remaining ingredients. Pour the dressing over the salad and stir well.

Serve the herring salad with boiled potatoes or black bread.

Plum dumplings

Plums are sweet and juicy. You can eat them fresh or try out a lot of recipes: The plums are often used in jam-making. Another favorite is preparing wine or liqueur with plums. A popular one is the Slivovitz, a plum brandy. In Germany and Austria, plums are often used for desserts and cakes. One famous recipe are the plum dumplings:

(4 servings)

1 lb.(damson) plums

juice of 1 lemon

2 tablespoons sugar

1 cinnamon stick

rum

1/1/2 lb. potatoes

1 lb. curd cheese

2/3 cup flour

2 tablespoons semolina

1 tablespoon butter

salt, nutmeg

Pit the plums and cut them into pieces. In a pot, combine the plums, the lemon juice, the sugar and the cinnamon stick. Over a medium heat, let it simmer for about 30 minutes. Then purée the plums and season, depending on taste, with rum.

Peel and cook the potatoes. Rice the potatoes and mix it up with all the other ingredients. Season with a dash of salt and a dash of nutmeg. Put the potato dough into the fridge for 30 minutes.

Depending on how big the dumplings should be, divide the dough into equal pieces. Bead the pieces, press in troughs with your thumbs. Fill the dumplings with the plum puree. Then close the dumplings.

Bring a big pot of water to a boil. Add a dash of salt, 1 tablespoon sugar and 1 tablespoon rum. Let the dumplings simmer for about 15 minutes.

Serve the dumplings warm with vanilla sauce.

You can also mix up 2 tablespoons of ground hazelnuts, 1 tablespoon of sugar and 1 teaspoon of cinnamon. Besprinkle the dumplings with the mixture.

Fruit cake

Dried fruits have a residual moisture of about 20 %. Ripe fruits, whole or cut into slices, are slowly dried by a minor heat supply. Because of the torrefaction the fruits lose moisture and gain in sugar content. In this way, you can keep the fruits longer. Often used are apples, pears, plums, wine (raisins) and apricots. You can also dry Southern Fruits, like figs and dates. Newly, exotic fruits are on offer; for example mangos and pineapples. Dried fruits are a main ingredient for the fruit cake:

(9x5 inch)

1/2/3 cup flour

1 tablespoon baking powder

1/2 cup sugar

salt

4 oz. butter

1 egg

1/4 cup milk

1 teaspoon rum extracts

1/4 teaspoon ground nutmeg

1/4 teaspoon ground clove

1/4 teaspoon ground cinnamon

zest of 1 lemon

1/3 cup candied orange peel

2/3 cup walnuts, hacked

1 cup dried figs, cut into pieces

1 cup dried apricots, cut into pieces

1 cup dried plums, cut into pieces

1/2 cup dried cranberries

For the dough, batter the sugar, a dash of salt and the butter, until you get a bright and smooth mixture. Stir in the egg. Sieve the flour and the baking powder into a bowl. Combine it with the mixture. Add the milk and the rum extracts.

Add the spices and the lemon peel to the dough and combine everything well.

At least, mingle the dough with the candied orange peel, the nuts and the dried fruits. Oil a loaf pan (9x5 inch) and pour the dough into it.

Preheat the oven at 375 °F. Bake the fruit cake for about 70 to 80 minutes.

Ham wrapped chicory with béarnaise sauce

Endive is a leaf vegetable. It has a fine bitter aroma. It is grown completely underground without any sunlight. The plant only shows the very tip of the leaves. The darkness prevents the leaves from turning green and opening up. This is why only the tips of the leaves are a little bit green. They are closer to the sunlight. As its name implies, endive grows in Belgium. The harvest is between September and November. Belgium exports the endives in about 40 different countries worldwide. Belgian endives can be cooked, steamed or used raw in salads.

(4 servings)

4 egg yolks

1 yellow onion, minced

8 oz. unsalted butter, melted

3/4 oz. tarragon, minced

salt

3/4 oz. parsley, minced

8 peppercorns, crushed

6 Belgian endives

2 teaspoon white wine vinegar

6 slices cooked ham, halved

3 tablespoon dry white wine

1 tablespoon water

In a saucepan, combine the onions, the herbs, the peppercorns, the vinegar, the white wine and the water. Bring the mixture to a boil and let it simmer for about 5 minutes. Put the saucepan off the range and let the mixture steep for another 20 minutes. Then strain the mixture and keep the reduction.

Blanch the endives for 3 minutes in salted boiling water. Then refresh them. Cut the endives into halves and cut the stems off. Wrap each half into one slice of cooked ham. Place the ham wrapped endives into a casserole.

Preheat the oven at 425 °F

For the béarnaise sauce, whisk the egg yolks and the reduction over a double boiler, until the mixture is creamy. Put it off the heat and beat in the melted butter. Season to taste with salt. Pour half of the sauce over the casserole. Broil it 5 to 7 minutes. Serve with the remaining sauce and boiled potatoes.

December 21st

Small nut wedges

The pecan nut resembles a walnut. The nuts have a rich and buttery flavor. On the other hand, almonds have a unique sweet flavor. Both kinds of nuts can be kept cool in the fridge or in the freezer. The excellent flavors are a fantastic combination for the small nut cakes. They give the cakes a great nutty flavor.

(32 pieces)

3/4 cup flour

1/2 teaspoon baking powder

1/4 cup sugar

1 teaspoon vanilla extract

1 egg

1/4 cup unsalted butter

3 oz. butter

1/2 cup honey

1 tablespoon natural Vanilla Sugar

2 tablespoons water

3 oz. ground pecans

3 oz. hacked pecans

4 oz. hacked almonds

5 oz. dark chocolate

1/4 cup peach jam

In a large bowl, combine the flour, the baking powder, the sugar, the vanilla, the egg and the butter. Knead a cookie dough. Add a little bit more flour, if the dough still sticks to the fingers. Wrap the cookie dough into plastic wrap and put it into the fridge for 1 hour. Then roll the dough on baking paper, in the size of a baking pan (16 x 12 x 1). Then move the dough onto the baking pan.

Brush the cookie dough with the peach jam.

Preheat the oven at 375°F

In a saucepan, warm the butter, the honey, the Vanilla Sugar and the water. Stir in the nuts and let the mixture cool down a little bit. Then spread the dough with the nuts mixture. Bake the cake for 20 to 25 minutes. Let it cool down.

Cut the cake into 16 squares. Cut each square diagonal in two triangles. Melt the chocolate and coat the edges of the small nut wedges with chocolate. Let the chocolate dry on a cooling rack.

Sauerkraut stew

Cinnamon is one of the oldest spices on the world (colorable 3000 BC). The seasoning is made from the bark of the cinnamon trees: the dried bark becomes rolled and later, it becomes cut into pieces, the cinnamon sticks. You can also buy ground cinnamon. Cinnamon is one of the most outstanding spices in Christmastime. The aromatic smell and the special taste are unmistakable. Cinnamon is versatile: You can bake with cinnamon, cook sweet meals or hearty and tasty dishes. Here is one sample for it.

(6 servings)

1/1/2 lb. pork shoulder, fat trimmed

1 teaspoon salt

2 bay leaves

3 cloves garlic, minced

3 cinnamon sticks

2 cups canned diced tomatoes, drained

1 lb. yukon gold potatoes, peeled and cubed

1 lb. sauerkraut, rinsed and drained

2/3 cup yellow onions, hacked

1/4 cup flour

salt, pepper

1 bunch Italian parsley, hacked

In a big pot, combine the pork shoulder, the salt, the bay leaves, the garlic and the cinnamon sticks. Pour at least 12 cups cold water over it. The meat should be covered completely. Bring it to a boil.

Let it simmer over a medium heat for about 2 hours.

After 1 hour add the tomatoes.

After another 30 minutes add the potatoes, the sauerkraut and the yellow onions. Stir well.

At the end of the cooking time remove the pork shoulder and cut it into bite-sized cubes. Then add the cubes to the stew.

Sprinkle the flour over the stew and stir constantly until the flour has expanded. Season the stew to taste with salt and pepper and stir in the hacked parsley.

Pomegranate - punch muffins

The circulation area of the **pomegranate** lies is the western to middle Asia. In the Mediterranean Area, and also in the Middle East the pomegranate is cultivated since several centuries. The harvest is from September to December. The pomegranates taste fruity and are very juicy. Pomegranate juice is popular all over the world, as well as the pomegranate syrup, which is a main ingredient for the "Tequila Sunrise" and other cocktails. In the eastern Mediterranean Area the pomegranate is used for fruit salads or green salads. They are also a main ingredient for meat -, poultry and rice meals.

(16 muffins)

1 cup flour

2 teaspoons baking powder

1 teaspoon baking soda

2 teaspoons cinnamon

2 tablespoons cacao

2 eggs

2/3 cup sugar

1/3 cup vegetable oil

2/3 cup red wine

1/3 cup buttermilk

1 tablespoon rum aroma

3 oz. almonds, hacked

4 oz. bittersweet chocolate, rasped

2 egg whites, salt

2 tablespoons sugar

2 tablespoons powdered sugar

1 teaspoon corn starch

1/2 cup ground almonds

1 pomegranate, opened-up

In a large bowl, combine all the dry ingredients.

In a mixing bowl, beat the eggs. Add the sugar and mix well. Add all the other ingredients. Stir in the almonds and the rasped chocolate.

Finally, stir in the dry ingredients.

Preheat the oven at 350 ˚F

Place baking cups into a muffin tray. Pour in the dough, about 2/3.

Bake them for 15 minutes. Meanwhile, beat the egg whites with a dash of salt. Add the sugar and the powdered sugar. When the mixture is very stiff, add also the starch. Finally, fold in the ground almonds and the pomegranate seeds.

Spread the whipped egg whites on the pre-baked muffins. Bake them for another 15 minutes. Let them cool down.

Sourdough bread with orange butter

Oranges are widely grown in warm climates worldwide. America is one of the top orange producers. You can peel and eat them; you can squeeze and drink them; or you can just use the orange zest for baking or cooking. The zest will give the dish a wonderful orange flavor. The flavor of oranges vary from sweet to sour. All in all, you can use the orange multilateral. Try out the salty orange butter with the sourdough bread.

(2 loaves of bread)

1 cup warm water

1 teaspoon honey

1 package dry yeast

1 cup whole wheat flour

1 cup whole wheat flour

1/2 cup warm water

1/2 teaspoon honey

1 cups whole wheat flour

2 cups bread flour

1 teaspoon salt

1 package dry yeast

1/3 cup warm water

sunflower seeds

4 oz. unsalted butter, soft

zest of 1 orange

salt

To prepare the starter, whisk the water, the honey and the yeast. Sift the flour into it and stir well, until you get a smooth paste. Cover it with plastic wrap and leave it at room temperature for 24 hours.

To prepare the sponge, stir the flour, the water and the honey into the starter, until you get a smooth mixture. Cover it and leave it again for 24 hours.

To prepare the dough, sift the flour into a bowl. Add the salt and the yeast. Mix everything well. Make a well in the centre. Pour the water into it. Add also the sponge mixture to the dry ingredients. Knead well, until the ingredients are incorporated. Place the dough in a lightly oiled bowl and cover it with a towel. Prove, until the dough is doubled in size. Knead for 1 minute. Then bisect the dough and shape the halves oval.

With a knife, cut several times diagonal 1/2 inch deep along both loaves.

Strew the sunflower seeds over the loaves, if desired.

Place them on a lightly floured baking tray. Cover them with a towel and prove the dough for another 30 minutes. Preheat the oven at 375°F.

Bake the bread for 35 to 40 minutes.

Mix up the butter and the orange zest. Season to taste with salt. Serve the orange butter with the sourdough bread.

Honey cake with Lumumba

Today, the different kinds of **honey** hail from the entire world. Honey is a sweetener, which is used since the Stone Age. The smell and the taste from honey is natural and pure. The following recipe has his origin in Europe; Germany and Denmark. The dough of the honey cake is like the gingerbread. Also, several ingredients are similar. The honey cake is a tradition at Christmastime.

Lumumba

(4 cups)

4 cups milk

1/2 cup sweet ground chocolate

4 cl. rum

1 cup whipped cream.

Warm the chocolate milk. Pour 1 cl. rum in each glass. Pour the hot chocolate over it. Garnish each glass with whipped cream.

Honey cake with Lumumba

(16 x 12 x 1)

1 cup honey

2/3 cup unsalted butter

1/4 teaspoon ground cloves

1 teaspoon cinnamon

a pinch of nutmeg

1 teaspoon rum

3 eggs

1/1/2 cups flour

2 teaspoons baking powder

1/1/2 teaspoons baking soda

1/2 cup ground walnuts

2 tablespoons blackberry jam

8 oz. white chocolate

1 tablespoon coconut oil

4 oz. semi-sweet chocolate

1 teaspoon coconut oil

Melt the butter and the honey in a saucepan. Pour it into a mixing bowl and let it cool down.

Preheat the oven at 350 °F

Then beat in the spices and the rum. After it, stir in the eggs, one at a time. Mix up the flour, the baking powder, the baking soda and the ground walnuts. Mix the flour-mixture with the honey-butter-mixture. Oil a rectangular baking pan and pour the cake dough into it, spread the dough well. Bake the cake for about 20 minutes.

Spread the cake immediately with the blackberry jam. Let it cool down.

Melt the chocolates in two different pots. Add the coconut oil to each pot. Brush the honey cake with the white chocolate. Fill the dark chocolate in an airtight bag. Cut off one little edge. Use the self-made piping bag to spread parallel lines on the honey cake. Now, use a bamboo skewer to draw lines crosswise. Change the direction after each line. In this way, you will get the nice patterns. Put the honey cake in the fridge until serving.

Happy Holidays

&

Happy New Year

CPSIA information can be obtained
at www.ICGtesting.com
Printed in the USA
LVHW070743091120
671136LV00001B/3